A Nation Under Siege

Political Discourse in America

Adrian L. Lawrence

ISBN: 978-0-578-90119-0

A Nation Under Siege: *Political Discourse in America*

CONTENTS

DEDICATION

I dedicate this book to my wife, Yasmin, and our sons, Adrian Jr. and Damian. Their encouragement and support over these years have been exceptional. They have encouraged me and provided the impetus and energy necessary to complete this project.

Foreword

Dr. Dennis V. Burke

Here is a book expressing the observation of the silent majority who expect more from our democracy. But who feels disappointed with the pessimism and constant political intransigence that is infecting the American optimism and way of life. The candid discussion and comparisons to the eighties experience in a developing country are an alarm bell, calling us all to action.

Preface

Political Discourse in America - A Nation Under Siege ®

In writing this book, I am aware that politics, social issues, and government are controversial areas to pursue in a society fraught with the practices of cancel culture. Still, I am obliged to initiate a dialogue on the issues contributing to a mean-spirited political discourse in our communities. This mean-spiritedness has been a significant factor in dividing the people of our nation.

Obviously, discussions about politics in America can potentially produce adverse outcomes. However, a true American citizen cannot adopt a cowardly posture and be afraid to speak out on fundamental issues in "the land of the free and home of the brave." Therefore, one must advocate reinstating a culture where we can express our opinions without fear of reprisals from individuals with different views. The deterioration in our ability to communicate or conduct political discourse is directly attributed to our collective inability to address social, economic, and structural inequalities.

We must respect the right of people to be different. Camille Kouchner once wrote, "If you do not speak, you leave an upside-down world." Our democracy is under intense threat. If we want to save our democracy from those who are counting on its demise, then we as citizens cannot surrender the right to speak or be different. We must take risks as necessary to save and preserve our democracy. Kouchner also argued that we ought to protect our democracy because we have a slight chance of saying to those who suffer that their suffering will account for something.

Years of social and political neglect provided the fuel for the events that led to the January 6, 2021 insurrection. My distaste for 21st-century political discourse, coupled with our society's continued polarization by leading politicians, and the blatant disregard for human intelligence, has produced the adrenaline necessary to write this book.

Although our political process resists extreme ideals, our Constitution and our democracy allow us the right to express ourselves without fear. We should not have to worry about being intimidated by people who abhor the truth. The truth is simply a collection of facts that reflects reality. It should be the primary standard we collectively use to operate in our democracy. However, some people insist on advocating for "alternative facts," and such a construct harms our society and must be rejected. Therefore, the advocacy of "alternative facts" and the wanton revision of history must be scrutinized and rejected.

Some will argue that the Constitution needs to be updated to reflect a new era, and perhaps they are right. But we must only attempt to update our Constitution through the legal means afforded us. Our Constitution is a public value and should be revised only with public participation and the majority's interest. I argue that as imperfect as the Constitution is, it might not be appropriate, nor is now the opportune time to make such revision. The people in our democracy are angry that we have lost our sense of compromise. Therefore, any modifications to the Constitution might reflect the concerns of groups with the most influence. Changes to the Constitution must be carefully considered, debated, and free of political, religious, and social banter.

My goal is to highlight how some of our citizens have chosen to ignore our constitutional rights by orchestrating various schemes calculated to silence people with different points of view. Many of these social and political strategies are promoting selfish draconian ideas of a select few. Solutions to the issues that I have outlined may be challenging to achieve given the current environment. As a nation, we cannot turn a blind eye to the challenges that we face; we must overcome these challenges. I hope that we can come together again as one nation under God with the ultimate goal of bringing much relief to a nation in turmoil.

Chapter 1

Motivation Through Early Political Education

As a teenager on the island of Jamaica, I watched citizens, whom I referred to as political junkies, conduct verbal assaults on each other under the umbrella of a political movement. I was fortunate to have a front-row seat at some public events because my parents operated a small grocery store in the village square. For a while, political tribalism and mean-spirited behavior appeared to be the norm. But when the level of discourse became personal and sometimes led to violence, I had difficulty accepting it as a norm.

Even at a young age, I had difficulty accepting the self-destructive model of political discourse that was popular in Jamaica. In my late teens, political violence took on a new meaning with carefully coordinated events that brought the country to the brink of economic and social disaster. The arguments and actions of politicians became painfully vindictive. They were aimed solely at gaining and keeping power at any cost. In the late 1970s, political discourse, misinformation, and violent retributive politics provided the framework for a significant social and economic meltdown.

The political process at the time and the culture became enshrined in class warfare, corruption, and cronyism. To my disappointment, I now realize that American politics has many similarities to the Jamaican political system. Still, the American political system has become exponentially worse than what I experienced in

Jamaica in the late seventies. However, there has never been a time when Jamaicans failed to have a peaceful transfer of power after an election. Despite political violence, especially in the late seventies and early eighties, and despite a high level of political and tribal conflict, in the end, the winning party has always had a peaceful transition into power.

The events of January 6, 2021, have caused me to be equally disappointed by the change in the American political culture that influences citizens to invade the U.S. Capitol with actions aimed at delegitimizing the process to certify a duly elected president. America now shares a culture of lies, racism, ideological confluence, and the resulting manipulation of its citizens. This movement of misinformation and disinformation is led by a few powerful and well-connected individuals who have access to the channels of communications. In some instances, the media helps promote the fallacy in search of ratings, "Breaking News." I want to emphasize that the disruption that I experienced growing up in Jamaica lacked racism, xenophobia, and outright sexism. The civil conflict in Jamaica was predicated on ideological misinformation and the dichotomy between political beliefs. Jamaica was a proxy battleground in the conflict between Soviet/Cuban socialist expansion and American capitalism.

America was established with prayer and faith being the bedrock of our strength and our democracy. Our coins and notes are engraved with the words "In God We Trust." In the last 30 years, I have observed every president conclude the most important speeches and address the nation with the words "May God Bless America." Yet, politicians are afraid to defend the principles on which this country was established. Instead, they have laid the foundations for new and destructive pillars that weaken our democracy. They have avoided taking a position on prayers in schools. They have not taken a position on "Merry Christmas" because they fear the political backlash.

What can we do to cleanse the landscape? We can peacefully take back our country from the well-connected, controlling local, state, and federal governments. Taking back our country means voting politicians out of office and replacing them with men and women with noble character. We must elect leaders who are committed to serving our country and its citizens and not themselves or some obscure political beliefs. We must reject the ideologies preached and instilled by the lobbyists who represent extreme right and left-wing causes. A term limit is an option. The citizens of the country retain the legal rights to recall and remove the benchwarmers and non-performing politicians.

Benchwarmers are congressional welfare recipients who are masquerading as representatives of the American people. Now is the time to be prepared to act in the next electoral cycle. The representatives who do not serve the people's needs should be sent home. They should forfeit severance and have restrictive covenants that limit corporate kickback for favors done while in office. We must insist and enforce; we must demand principle-based character in our representatives. We must punish officials at the ballot box whenever they habitually violate the trust of the people.

Chapter 2

Political and Social Dilemma

The political process in the United States is more maligned than the political system and process in Jamaica. Jamaican politicians practiced "pork-barrel politics" by providing food for the less fortunate during an election cycle. They fed pork to the people but often forgot that the people existed after the ballots were tabulated. Conversely, in the U.S., pork is doled out daily through legal means, such as placing political cronies in high offices controlled by powerful politicians, surrogates, and lobbyists. We recall that U.S. politicians have built bridges to nowhere. Our nation continues the pervasive handout of corporate welfare to friends and families while ignoring the critical social issues facing our country. These actions only serve to disenfranchise the citizens of America and over the years, have provided fuel for anger and promoted social dislocation.

Political and social unrest in America did not happen overnight. The disruption and political chaos we are experiencing are merely the culmination of years of inaction by both political parties. After reflecting on my political upbringing, my early conclusion was that the fractured political climate I experienced in Jamaica could never be replicated in the United States. I assumed that the American democracy was a mature and sophisticated political culture. Obviously, I miscalculated the extent of the political perils in America. I missed signs of a fractured culture trying to escape the wrongs of slavery. I never thought that we would have leaders calling our citizens awful names, referring to countries from which immigrants came as "Shit-Hole Countries." I have always believed that America's diversity is its strength.

Under the current construct, we have not solved America's problems, and the list is growing. We have the lowest graduation rates from our colleges than other developed nations and the lowest minimum wage, just to name a few. To those who believe that addressing these issues is akin to socialism, I say that the so-called socialist policies are less disruptive. They are less expensive than the alternatives because we have seen the level of social and economic disruption explode within the last four years. When we address social inequities, we will reduce homelessness, solve the healthcare crisis, address the lack of affordable housing, and curb civil disturbances and social disobedience. We might also discourage fringe groups and political leaders from fermenting hate and distrust in our society.

Long before the pandemic reached our shores, America, the world's wealthiest nation, had more than half a million homeless people. Homelessness has cost cities and states billions of dollars to house and keep the homeless off our cities' streets. Homelessness in our country has been compounded because the federal government has long abandoned building public housing for low-income residents. Congress is fully aware that the private sector will not build low-income housing because of marginal financial returns from these projects. For too long, Congress and the government's executive branches have turned a blind eye to this issue. Over an extended period, like a volcano getting ready to erupt, social inequities have been bubbling up, and this eruption will contribute to a social and economic tsunami.

Another issue contributing to social unrest in this country is that the federal minimum wage has remained at seven dollars and twenty-five cents per hour for more than a decade. The minimum wage has remained stagnant while housing costs have risen significantly, especially in major urban cities. A combination of the above has led to disappointment and disillusionment in the people. It has contributed to a lack of participation in the social and economic agenda and low voter participation.

The insurrection of January 6' 2021, was not a mirage. It was real, and the current administration has one more chance to address some underlying issues. If they don't, another Trump-like character will be elected president. He or she may succeed in motivating the disenfranchised people in future insurrections. Americans deserve the birth of a new age, an age when we undergo the cleansing of white supremacy and other social ills from our shores. We need a voice of compassion that recognizes our weaknesses and pain and seeks ways to heal the pain and heal America.

The conduct of parents and adults, in general, is vital in the pursuit of respectful political discourse. If we are to bridge the gap in this politically unstable climate, people must engage and speak up. Our kids and young adults watch our every move; they listen to what we say and how we say it. We must conduct ourselves in a manner that will have a positive influence on our kids. Dorothy Law Nolte, Ph.D., wrote the famous poem, "Children Learn What They Live," a quote that tells the story. It is our duty as a civilized society to leave a positive legacy for our kids to emulate. If we do not conduct ourselves appropriately, our kids will emulate our misdeeds, and the struggle for the soul of America will continue.

Other social and political issues that have affected America's political discourse include voter suppression and gerrymandering of electoral lines. Each party is obsessed with ensuring its control of power. According to the Brennan Center, some states such as Pennsylvania have begun mapping their judicial system into electoral districts to complicate matters. A select few carry out the level of activities surrounding the retention of power in the electorate's purview. These are the kinds of structural tinkering that have angered so many, providing a perfect set of circumstances for someone like Trump to manipulate and thrive. Trump will not be the last if these selfish acts continue.

The U.S., the wealthiest country on earth, has more than 10 million American children living in poverty. These children are deprived of vital resources and opportunities for advancement. In most developed countries, there are programs to help the children who live in poverty. If we continue to ignore poverty, Americans will pay a significant price in the end. It is not surprising that America has the highest rate of incarceration compared to other developed countries.

Americans proudly focus on the nation's wealth, although the wealth is concentrated in the top 1 percent of the population. We cannot wish away our problems. If we continue to ignore social issues and pretend that they do not exist in our "city on a hill," then our perceived success will be just an illusion. We must be cognizant that there are also cities in the valleys of America just beneath those glorious cities on the hills. If the cities in the valleys are given the right level of attention, the socio-economic conditions that are present in these communities will be improved. If our government officials think that it will cost too much to fix social inequities, it will cost much more in the future when our kids become adults. Imagine a future in which a significant segment of the population has substandard education and limited skills; this is a prescription for social disaster and the classic description of underdevelopment.

A prolonged colossal failure of government and society spanning several administrations has paved the way for white supremacists and other fringed groups to expand their operations. This neglect has given birth to QAnon, Oath Keepers, Proud Boys, Antifa, and Trumpism. Our nation has seen far-right, anti-government organizations composed of current and former military and police who, independent of the citizens of this country, pledge to fulfill their oath to "defend the Constitution against all enemies." Interestingly enough, the chairman of the Proud Boys plans to run for elective office.

Fringe groups prosper not because they are solving or attempting to solve societal problems. They thrive because they observe how American corporations and corporations worldwide have traditionally treated the working class. Employees have often felt that they have done tremendous work and have not gotten the corporate and financial recognition they deserve.

The gap between executive compensation and the salaries of ordinary workers has increased exponentially. David Gelles wrote an article in the *New York Times* in which he reported that chief executives of major companies made on average 320 times more than their employees. For example, he mentioned that Hilton laid off almost a quarter of its staff, lost $720 million, but the chief executive received approximately $60 million in compensation. In the fiscal year 2020, Norwegian Cruise Lines lost $4 billion, furloughed more than 20 percent of its staff, but doubled the payment to its chief executive to $36.4 million.

In contrast, workers sitting at home unemployed and virtually bankrupt strongly feel that executive management should share financial hardships and not receive such levels of compensation during a crisis. These actions taken by the executive management and the boards of major corporations propel people worldwide to seek relief elsewhere. Feeling overwhelmed and out of place, they tend to join groups like QAnon, Oath Keepers, and others.

There have been unprecedented worldwide recruiting efforts by these fringe groups. QAnon has seen significant growth across the globe and has grown exponentially in Japan. The people and government of Japan are concerned about the rapid growth of these groups, considering the speed at which their country has adopted QAnon.

The events of January 6, 2021, were no accident; instead, it was an accident waiting to happen. The circumstances were inevitable due to social and economic injustices mixed with misinformation, disinformation, and bad politics. I recognize that Congress and some Americans feel that helping the poor, the less fortunate, and people who are experiencing short-term difficulties is tantamount to supporting socialist policies. Unless we address our country's significant issues, we will continue to see more social and political disruption. These disruptions will render permanent damage to the social and economic fabric of our nation.

Chapter 3

A Nation Under Siege

The idea of America has been a country rooted in Christianity for most of its history. This American idea is about upholding a doctrine that requires each of us to love our neighbors, help the weak if we are strong, and respect one another. Still, religious activists and members of the political right, through their actions, have sown the seeds of discord, creating fear and resentment in its citizens' hearts. America's system of governance has left too many citizens in despair and too many unresolved social and political issues. Our government is controlled by lobbyists, special interest groups, and corporations. The government is subjected to the archaic rules that govern the House and Senate; rules of convenience designed to ensure lifetime job security. Lawmakers at both the local and federal levels are interested in preserving their seats in the respective legislature. They have shown little interest in addressing the issues that affect their constituents.

Our nation is under siege because a minority of its citizens have refused to understand and accept that we are a diverse nation. Diversity brings differences of opinions, conduct, and religious beliefs, to name a few. Our country is supposed to be the melting pot of all nations. Instead, we appear to be more intolerant of each other, and the booming melting pot is close to a meltdown. There may be economic and commercial benefits to be gained from encouraging divisiveness. However, propaganda and ignorance are the recipes for chaos, such as the recent insurrection. We are so polarized that we have moved to politicize the COVID-19 vaccination campaign. The success of this program is a matter of life or death. The central question is how do we get to be a nation that will realize Martin Luther King Jr.'s dream? That dream seems to be severely under stress and under siege.

The religious right, the ultra-right-wing media, and Ivy League-educated bigots have created an un-American atmosphere. They have done this by creating a scenario in which there is no room for differences of opinions or beliefs. These groups have a value system predicated on the slogan "My Way or the Highway." We no longer agree to disagree. Instead, we strive to punish our perceived enemies who happen to have a difference of opinion from ours and often employ cancel culture. These groups are promoters of the zero-sum game. If we practice an eye-for-an-eye politics, eventually, everyone will be blinded and not able to participate in the development of our country.

Political parties, members of Congress, and the legislatures no longer have constructive debates or foster reconciliation of issues on behalf of "We the People." Members of our government, both local and federal, seek to intimidate other members with good intentions by erecting all plausible roadblocks dictated by special interest groups and lobbyists. Our elected officials' only concern is to be re-elected, even if it means selling their souls for political contributions.

Elected officials have joined forces with religious operatives who define abortion as the only "Sin" while turning a blind eye to other atrocities. To these individuals, murder, rape, stealing, etc., are not considered sins as severe as abortion. When employees toil for fifty hours per week and remain in poverty, we have a sin that masks slavery. They have agreed that abortion is taking a life but conclude that capital punishment is acceptable. In other words, a valuable life was not lost by hanging. Therefore, no protest. A life taken by lethal injection is somehow different than a life taken by abortion. For several years, Americans have seen their communities devasted by gun violence. But, some of the preservers of the status quo remain silent, while others rationalize societal behavior. When American kids are gunned down in schools and in the streets, we as a society do not express the level of outrage as in cases of abortion.

Disagreements are healthy for our democracy, but when we disagree, we should respect the context of our disputes and avoid letting our conflicts divide us. Our point of view should be predicated on facts and not necessarily the outcome each of us desires. Recall that Columbus was convinced that the world was flat. Still, as he explored the world, the facts became evident that the world was indeed round. He smartly accepted the obvious. Columbus did not conjure up devious schemes to support his original beliefs, nor did he go on tirades to promote unsupported personal positions; he accepted facts. Therefore, for our nation to succeed, we may need to learn **how** to learn. Throughout the ages, people who have learned from the facts have changed the nature of human existence.

Our country as a whole is under siege because our mindset,

political will, decency, and kindness to each other have fallen to a new low. We need to start loving our neighbor as ourselves, even when we disagree with each other. Our democracy is under siege, and I must confess that I do not have all the answers for all of the issues that I intend to examine in this book, but we must work together to save our democracy and our country. The days of the Wild West should be put behind us forever because fighting for the crumbs falling off the table will not give any of us the comparative advantage that we seek. We will succeed only when we respect each other, recognize our differences, and solve problems together because that's the only way we will win and realize a fair and just union.

Chapter 4

Political Representation by Manipulation

In an article published in the Indiana Law Journal, Alfred De Grazia states, "Representation is the crux of the relationship between public and republic; between the people and their Government. It is rather surprising and unfortunate that so little has been done by way of a systematic analysis of the theory and practice of Representation in the United States." Politicians are no longer representing their constituents; they are interested in securing stature and power. Their actions have become a reality show of sorts.

Some promote their Ivy League education. They are the so-called "smart men." They are an elite group that we, the people, dare not criticize or vote against. The question is, what have they done for "We the People" lately, if ever? America still has a shortage of affordable houses and dilapidated roads, airports, and bridges. We lack access to consistently good healthcare. We have increasing poverty and an aging, unreliable system of public transportation. Politicians spend an excessive amount of time on political maneuvering and deception rather than on addressing the crucial issues that face the nation. Their responsibilities as public officials are not aligned with the desires of the people that they represent.

The transformation of Congress to a new paradigm began under Newt Gingrich when he joined Congress in 1979. His goal was to shake up and radicalize Congress by being mean-spirited and disruptive to members of Congress. In 1983, Gingrich founded the Conservative Opportunity Society, which in 1994 produced the

"Contract with America." Little did Americans realize that this contract was a one-sided proposition benefitting only Gingrich. Long before the Internet and the birth of social media, Gingrich weaponized C-Span to reach his intended audience.

For decades, America has been recognized as the bastion of democracy and decency, perceived as a model that the world should emulate. Still, our leaders in Congress and the White House have placed love of country and the Constitution on the backburner. At the same time, they pursued and experimented with ideological toys. In the eyes of a few, the Constitution has become a document of convenience. We should use the Constitution if it aligns with our objectives and world views, and it should be ignored when it works against us.

The perks of being in Congress or the White House appear to be more important to politicians than working on behalf of the people. Make no mistake, America, as it stands, is like an aircraft carrier fully loaded with stealth aircraft and armed nuclear missiles, heading to and blinded by the proverbial iceberg. The path to the iceberg was not one directed by the military leadership. Still, this vessel has been hacked and hijacked by right-winged, white supremacists and self-preserving politicians and operatives, leaving the current administration struggling to regain control.

Chapter 5

Seeing Through the Political Lenses

Americans increasingly view the country through opaque political lenses. What they are seeing has made them frustrated and disenchanted with the political system. More Americans are changing their political affiliation to unaffiliated or independent than at any time in our history. These changes are because our citizens have become disillusioned by the conduct of the two major political parties. Still, Republicans and others have elevated their game and have taken the abuse to a new level. The people of this country are incredibly disappointed by what they have experienced in the last four years of the Trump Administration.

The ex-president has chosen to demonize and mock the very people who elected him to power. These are the same citizens who continue to pay the salaries and provide other top-flight benefits to the administration and congressional members. Several years ago, a group of individuals desperate to send a message to both political parties resulted in the birth of the Tea Party. In other instances, citizens have joined ultra-right winged groups or have become "Progressives." Tea Party leaders and others have adopted the same manipulative strategies of one of our major political parties. I believe that these collations will self-destruct, as evident with the Tea Party movement and its predecessor led by Gingrich under the umbrella of his so-called "Contract with America."

Most political candidates, local and national, are only interested in retaining power at any cost. They seek long-term job opportunities in the House and Senate. These positions offer immense power, networking, a pulpit to showcase their wares, six-figure salaries, and excellent benefits. Ironically, politicians are in some instances afraid to vote on important issues for fear of constituent backlash and the possibility of facing another candidate in the primary election. These men and women are gutless citizens who have lost the ability to stand up for a principle regardless of the political cost. While they enjoy Congress's extravagances, many members of their constituencies sit with empty bowls waiting for a measure of soup, a meal that never came.

The rise of the progressives might be a blessing in disguise and might have produced positive outcomes. Generally, the progressives are aligned to the political left, leaving a void on the right. While I do not share all the progressives' views, I fully support their quest to address social inequality and environmental issues. This movement has lit a fire under the butts of lazy, ineffectual Congressmen and women. In addition to the progressive movement, big corporations are pulling back support after witnessing the insurrection on January 6, 2021. They are pushing for change in the political arena. Privately funded groups are also actively poised to influence change in the political process. This change is long overdue.

Chapter 6

Political Labels

Political labels are designed to play mind games with the people of this country and shame or praise individuals for their political views. Under this construct, being labeled a socialist carries a negative implication while being conservative is viewed by some in a positive light. Initially, we referred to our citizens as Democrats, Republicans, and Independents, transforming conservatives, ultra-conservatives, liberals, progressives, left, center, right, etc. None of these labels have solved America's problems. However, they have sown the seeds of discord and division. They have nurtured destructive political discourse, and these are some of the tools that politicians use to manipulate our people. Under the current operating philosophy, what an individual believes hardly matters in this climate; it's whom one supports.

Political labels also provide branding and fodder for political operatives and news organizations to exploit ordinary Americans' minds and well-being. Ronald Regan's "Supply Side" economics, Newt Gingrich's "Contract with America," and Donald Trump's "Make America Great Again" campaigns did very little to address the social and economic inequities of Americans. Neither have these political labels benefitted Americans in any tangible way. Instead, these slogans served to promote political egos and division, rather than solving the social and economic problems that presidents and members of Congress were elected to address. Many operatives, right-wing zealots, members of religious organizations, left-wing activists, and sympathizers attached themselves to these labels, much to our country's detriment.

Religious organizations have traditionally supported right-winged political operatives because they claim to support a single issue such as abortion, which I categorize as political witchcraft. I am not an advocate for abortion but encourage adoptions. Conversely, the folks who are opposed to abortion rights are not eagerly and vigorously supporting adoptions. Strangely enough, these religious organizations turned a blind eye to all other social issues. Looking back at the period when Catholic priests molested young boys, the clergy hid the facts and remained silent for many years, although they were most vocal on other social issues. As a Christian, I believe that "no sin will enter heaven," and the consequences of religious organizations' actions will leave them on the wrong side of the ledger and history.

While Americans label each other, critical issues such as poverty in America are on the rise. There is a lack of affordable housing, inadequate healthcare, failing schools, and dilapidated airports, and other infrastructures. We spend heavily on wars while neglecting the needs of our country. These are the issues that the people and their governments should be discussing instead of focusing on political branding. Politicians and religious organizations have not served the people well; instead, Congress members spend most of their time fundraising to keep themselves permanently in Congress. Churches have turned to prosperity doctrine as a means of diverting the focus from the real issues. The day is coming when we will all face the proverbial music for those who chose to digress.

Chapter 7

Political Indifference and Mis-information

Americans got themselves involved in a reckless social and political engagement when they elected Donald Trump. They elected Trump despite a warning from Michael Bloomberg, who spoke at the Democratic Convention. At the convention, Bloomberg explained why Trump was not fit for office. During the Republican primary, members of the Republican Party expressed similar views regarding Mr. Trump. Further, Trump's business record was in plain sight. Still, Americans fell for the allure of his fancy private jet, combative demeanor, and failed to recognize that they were going to bed with a man who is the master of misinformation. They thought instead that Hillary Clinton was the devil in disguise. Therefore, Trump and his army of conservatives and special interest groups promoted a campaign of misinformation with alleged support from Russian operatives. We may never know the extent to which foreign operatives participated in the election because sections of Mueller's report that deal with this issue have been redacted.

Throughout the Obama presidency and since he became president, Donald Trump has brilliantly used his access to media outlets. During his presidency, he has exploited the bully pulpit to lie and misinform Americans and the world. The sad irony is that Trump never cared to consider the pain he brought on others; he was only concerned about himself. As of December 31, 2020, it is estimated that Trump told more than 30,000 lies, 4,000 lies in October 2020 alone, according to an article written by Glen Kessler of Politico.

The campaign of lies and misinformation has done significant damage to the image and security of the United States. Trump promoted civil disobedience, advanced the practice of offering "alternative facts," and categorized information that may be damaging to him, his family, and surrogates as "Fake News." Because of Trump's actions, this once-revered nation now finds itself being compared with Nigeria or Russia.

Over the years, Trump's actions have polarized the country, splitting Americans into fractious groups. Members of these groups are committed to violence to achieve the desired outcome, even if it entails destroying our democracy. This behavior was evident in the January 6 attack on the Capitol compound in Washington D.C. During the January 6 assault, Trump, his allies, and enablers may have done irreparable damage to our democracy, the U.S. Constitution, and the Republican Party. The people who participated in Trump's grand lie about electoral fraud and those who supported storming the Capitol will be relegated to the annals of political purgatory.

Bob Woodward documented Trump's lies regarding the COVID 19 pandemic. Trump's actions and inactions directly or indirectly resulted in the deaths of more than half a million Americans in a country with just 4 percent of the world's population. His actions also dealt a long-term crippling blow to American business and the economy, a state of affairs that is expected to last deep into 2021. During the Trump era, people were scolded for being "politically correct." One is regarded as politically correct if one speaks the truth or conforms to societal norms. He also discouraged respectful conversations and instead encouraged brash, threatening, and disrespectful banter. He shamed and antagonized his opposition, disregarding the severe lingering effects that his actions may have on those who disagreed with him.

Chapter 8

Trumpism

Donald Trump did not run for president because he was inspired to serve the people of the United States. He ran because, like Boss Tweed, he "saw his opportunity and took them." His ultimate goal was not to "Make America Great Again," but instead, the slogan should read, "Make Trump Wealthy Again." Of course, being president and having the power of the presidency with control of the F.B.I., Justice Department, and military means he had almost total control of the nation and an uncanny ability to control significant decisions across the globe. "Trumpism" is the caricature of greed, distortion, lies, and the misrepresentation of American values.

The promulgation of these traits produces a social virus that may be harder to eradicate than COVID-19. Trump, a modern-day "pied piper," believes in the pageantry of being president but ignores the work and sacrifice necessary to perform the duties of the presidency. To add insult to injury, he surrounds himself with a cadre of wealthy, well-connected, incompetent characters. No person in the history of the world has successfully used social media as effectively as Trump to lie, threaten, deceive, and intimidate his adversaries, and "we the people" let him get away with it. However, he was impeached twice by the House of Representatives, although Trump suffered no consequences due to the impeachment.

Trump was born in Queens, New York, and over the years inherited wealth and real estate properties from his late father. He expanded the real estate business in New York and across the globe. Additionally, he dabbled in several other types of businesses, some of which were dismal failures. Today, he is persona-non-grata in New York because of how he treated the people of New York during his presidency. It's a sad moment when one is not welcomed in their place of birth.

As a man born with a perpetual gold spoon in his mouth, he recognized the plight of those who were disenfranchised. Therefore, he masqueraded himself as a savior of the disenfranchised. Donald Trump promised the working-class unequivocal relief and guaranteed positive outcomes. He was quoted as saying, "Only I can fix it." Many people accepted the notion that Trump cared for the plight of the working class, despite warnings from a real N.Y. multibillionaire, who described Trump as "known among millionaires as a con artist, and amongst business owners as a cheat out to stiff everyone." He exploited the poor's insecurities, the hungry, the disenfranchised, and the middle class and promised unspecified relief, and they fell for the deception. He mocked his opponents and the disabled, giving each pseudonym to demonize, diminish, and use the bully pulpit and social media to promote his venomous platform.

Trump enlisted members of Congress to assist with the promotion of his endless schemes of deception and lies. He threatened them with political extinction if they did not support his schemes and programs of deceit. During his presidency, he used the Justice Department and the F.B.I. as his office of war and disruption against his detractors. The weak and spineless yes men folded like caterpillars, the caterpillars that produce dangerous life-changing butterflies.

The checks and balances enshrined in the Constitution have not worked well during the Trump era. The presidency has now become an unchecked monarchy. The Justice Department has drafted and maintained archaic rules, not supported by the Constitution, that prevent a sitting president from prosecution. Further, Trump has used his powers to shield several of his associates from investigations and prosecutions. He has issued pardons and commuted sentences for hundreds of his friends and associates for an array of criminal activities. To that end, Congress needs to consider new laws to prevent a repeat of this abuse of power.

Trump courted right-winged extremists and gave them a voice. As a result, the message of hate engulfed America, waking up the evil forces of racism, bigotry, narcissism, and misogyny, evils that most Americans thought were buried in ancient history. He courted operatives, aligned himself to QAnon, a discredited far-right group, to carry out his disinformation and destruction mission in exchange for promises made. Still, typically he has reneged on his promises as Trump usually does.

Known as "The Big Lie," Trump conjured up a scheme that suggested large-scale voter fraud across the country in the 2020 elections. As a result, Trump initiated more than 50 election lawsuits in a few states. These lawsuits have either been settled, denied, withdrawn, or lost. However, Trump insisted that there were improprieties but did not produce the evidence to support his claim. The Big Lie was the fuel used to plan, ignite and execute the January 6, 2021 insurrection.

"We the People" must double our efforts to cleanse this disease from the shores of America. We can never accept the notion that an insurrection is a viable tool for changing our government and certainly not welcomed in our democracy. We cannot and should not embrace white nationalism in America. We need healthy political discourse with our neighbors without personalizing the exchange. We must cleanse America of the stain of Trumpism. By doing so, America will emerge a more tolerant and peaceful society. The road to the restoration of American values will be difficult if not exhaustive, but we cannot afford to keep our eyes off the prize. The cleansing starts now.

Chapter 9

Hate Speech

The first amendment protects freedom of speech. It can be described as the freedom to express opinions and ideas without fear of retaliation by others through censorship or legal actions. Hate speech is not protected or accepted in our country. According to the United States courts, freedom of speech also means not speaking, protesting, or using offensive words and phrases to convey political messages. Free speech also guarantees freedom of expression regardless of the medium used to disseminate that information. However, according to the U.S. courts, freedom of speech does not include the right to incite actions that would harm others or make or distribute obscene materials. Free speech does support hate speech, which expresses hatred for a particular group of people.

Generally, some people get involved or become aligned with hate groups and violence because they perceive that they are being left behind. Some people believe society may leave them behind or have left them altogether. Wealthy individuals rarely get directly involved in riots and public disturbances because they do not perceive that they were wronged by society. The underrepresented folks who struggle to make ends meet are more susceptible to being manipulated by individuals with significant influence.

The earliest form of social media was created in 1997. The white power movement led by Louis Beam, then the Grand Dragon of the Texas Chapter of the Ku Klux Klan, traveled with a Commodore 64 computer. However, the Internet was not general public knowledge until the early 1990s. During the Trump era, many Americans have been surprised at the rise in hate speech. However, this social disease has been around for a decade, hiding in the shadows of our democracy. Politicians and some media outlets have consistently encouraged the use of hateful speech. Most recently, Representative Marjorie Taylor-Green, a QAnon member, took hateful speech to another level, on the floor of the U.S. Congress. Much to my dismay, I discovered that some churches are supporters of hate groups like QAnon.

There are those in our society who manipulate others who are going through difficult times to promote hateful acts. The people who are being manipulated are vulnerable. They often conclude that their personal and social concerns have and will not be addressed. Therefore, they are easily influenced to conduct hateful and unlawful acts. This situation ordinarily gives rise to Trump-like figures, which generally promote hate. These Trumpians highlight the concerns of the manipulated, offering to rid them of their social and economic problems. Somehow these folks accept the idea that their problems result from the negligence of minorities and people of color, including Mexicans and people from other countries.

The wrong notion is being reinforced when the leadership model refers to minorities as criminals and rapists from "Shit Hole Countries." Trump and his mercenaries routinely tap into the general public's discontent, using their rage and anger with the system to encourage offensive language and outrageous behavior. These behaviors often lead to criminal activities, to which perpetrators conclude that there is no other way for their voices to be heard.

Hate speech by politicians has fueled unprovoked attacks on the Asian community in New York City and around the country. This community has been targeted, punched, kicked, and fatally shot for no apparent reason. There has been speculation that these attacks have been motivated by the former president whose speeches heavily criticize countries such as China. In many of the ex-president's speeches, he often labeled the COVID-19 virus as the "China Virus." Things have gotten so far out of control that older folks who are just taking a morning or evening stroll have been routinely harassed, beaten, and knocked to the ground. In a few instances, people of Asian descent have been attacked while awaiting trains on the New York City subway platforms. In Atlanta, nail salons operated by people of Asian descent were targeted, resulting in the death of eight individuals, including six people of Asian descent. For quite a while, our country has not seen this level of hostility against each other.

Rush Limbaugh, the purveyor of hate speech in this country, earned an estimated $80 million per year, peddling his wares and knowingly lying to the people. Lying has become a way of life that is engrained in the DNA. of Limbaugh and his enablers. Rush's stocks in trade have metastasized like cancer over the bodies of many of his followers. These men and women are peddlers of falsehood, failing to uphold the truth. They are purveyors of hate and are aware of the hurt they are inflicting on others. They have demonized an entire class of people and have earned boatloads of money in the process.

To suppress free speech and promote hate, the Republican party has chosen to censure members who disagree or criticize the leadership or state political apparatus. Families are being torn apart at an alarming rate as political discourse veers out of hand. Two days after Mr. Adam Kinzinger, the six-term Illinois congressman, called for the removal of President Trump from office, in response to the January 6 insurrection at the Capitol, the Illinois Republican Party moved to censure him. Political discourse is at an all-time low in America. News reports suggest that Mr. Kinzinger's family sent him a handwritten two-page letter that categorized him as being in support of "the devil's army." The text of the letter expands to include, "Oh my, what a disappointment you are to God and us," you have embarrassed the Kinzinger's family name." It is somewhat surprising and sad that a difference in opinion or personal beliefs can divide a family to the extent that this affected the Kinzinger family.

These purveyors of lies and misinformation have one thing in common: They make money and gain fame, and lots of it, at the expense of the citizens of this country. Some of the affected will never recover from the mental and psychological damage that was inflicted on them. According to an article in the *New York Times*, published on January 30, 2021, Roger Cohen reported that the president of France, in an interview with journalists, expressed his views on social media by stating that "Social media had brought about a kind of "anthropological mutation" characterized by "fascination with hatred." We must, as a nation, use every tool in our toolbox to eradicate this disease from our communities and our country.

Chapter 10

The Media

In the late '70s and early '80s, the primary forms of communication were print media, radio, and television. During this era and even today, these media platforms are somewhat regulated, primarily through government regulations and gentlemen's agreement between media companies and the public. As a result of these control mechanisms and quasi-contracts, there were fewer attempts to spread inaccurate information. Further, during this period, except radio and television, yesterday's news was the following day's headlines. Back then, a combination of attention to detail, and the natural delay in the process, made it more difficult to distribute information rapidly across broad geographical areas, not to mention overseas.

The Internet has revolutionized the distribution of news and information. It is a perfect vehicle in which purveyors of lies and misinformation can thrive. Data and information can be amplified and distributed across the world in seconds. Notwithstanding, key media outlets are constantly under attack by right-wing interest groups. The *New York Times* and *Washington Post* are constantly under attack for articles published based on investigative journalism. As you may recall, it was investigative journalism that brought down the Nixon Administration. Although these publications are often denounced as fake news, the opposing parties have not provided evidence to discredit their authenticity.

There is a fundamental difference between a journalist and a pundit. Journalists are charged with informing the public without injecting their positions or beliefs. They are expected to follow the facts. As a result, they build a level of trust between the journalist and the audience. Generally, we expect journalists to remain professionally impartial. Still, we know from experience that there is a tendency to introduce some bias in their reporting.

On the other hand, pundits and media influencers make us believe the improbable. Their tendency to often bend the truth creates confusion and sometimes supplants facts with opinions. Pundits often resort to cancel culture, but the victims of cancel culture are generally the marginalized and less powerful. The consequences of these actions to the affected parties are profound.

The oligopolization of the media has led to the American media's consolidation throughout most of the '80s and '90s. As a result, these actions have placed ultimate power in the hands of a few who do not necessarily represent Americans' ideals. Some elements of the American media suffer from willful blindness and generally refuse to cover critical newsworthy events. Their reporting appears to be in support of one of the two major political parties. Media is now being categorized as liberal, conservative, or right-wing, among other social labels. Wealthy individuals and corporations now control the primary channels by which the media operates. Since most media relies on advertising dollars to maintain operations, advertisers can use their business as leverage to support an idea or position. Today's journalists are paid extensive fees and salaries to host or appear on syndicated programs. Therefore, cable and network programming must generate significant advertising dollars to offset these overhead costs.

Unlike network television, the government did nothing to control the level of disinformation in our country over the years. I understand the Constitution's latitude to free speech and the government's position on free speech. However, the level of control over other forms of media is remarkably different from the standards imposed on network television. As a result, we have unleashed a social monster on the American public. The effects may be attributed to government's inaction. However, corporations have been affected by this campaign of disinformation and have decided to seek redress. Now they are suing the purveyors that promoted the disinformation against their corporation.

Corporations have the resources to address libelous behaviors. Still, many citizens cannot afford to litigate unjust charges leveled against them. A recent lawsuit filed by large corporations due to broadcast segments by the so-called conservative outlets were forced to hurriedly conduct damage control by terminating employees and changing specific programs' format. For example, Fox Business canceled its highest-rated show. Fox also began to moderate its broadcasts because of a $2.7 billion defamation lawsuit filed by an election technology company. Further, in response to legal actions, a guest appearing on Newsmax was cut off when he seemed to have crossed the newly temporarily established boundaries. These actions were too little too late.

Chapter 11

Social Media

Social media was designed to enable users to create and share information or participate in social networking forums and educate communities. The irony is that the U.S. invented the Internet and associated social media platforms. Still, state actors such as Russia and China have beaten us at our own game. With the introduction of social media, world communities assumed that there would be a level of honesty, civility, and decency in how we share information. We could not have imagined that the Internet would be weaponized to disrupt our civilization and potentially destroy our way of life, morally and physically. Now we have experienced instances where politicians, state-sponsored operatives, and more broadly, social media junkies weaponize social media platforms. They have turned a well-intentioned phenomenon into a forum with highly concentrated lies, character assassination, and misinformation. Despite the social hiccups, social media has made its mark in bringing news and information to people worldwide in record time.

In the U.S., bad actors hide behind the first amendment "Free Speech" clause to conduct outrageous acts. Some of the disgraceful content that is constantly disseminated over social media and cable TV could not be shared or broadcasted over radio and television networks. Social media has become a cesspool where people air dirty laundry instead of using this media to educate and positively influence each other. For several years, the status quo remained until our worst fears became a reality on January 6, 2021, the day that the world will remember as "Trump Insurrection Day." One could argue that the Trump-led insurrection was far more damaging to the nation than the act of domestic terrorism perpetrated by Timothy McVeigh in 1995. Recall that Mr. McVeigh was briefly a member of the Klan, and a friend of white supremacists, as is Trump.

Social media was the most critical tool used to organize, ignite, and direct the insurrection against the U.S. Capitol. The Congress and the executive branch of government have failed to curb the activities of those who perpetrate hateful language and outright lies to the public. The time has come when Congress and the executive branch must lead by example and establish operating standards for social media. Our government has set operational boundaries for other forms of media. Still, it did not attempt to develop similar boundaries for cable television and social media. It has been 25 years since a comprehensive internet regulation was passed. Congress needs to establish clear guidelines to address the current issues.

Supporters of free speech argue that social media should be left to operate the way it is to uphold free speech. Still, freedom of speech cannot be a prescription to lie, deceive, and promote demagoguery. Freedom of speech should maintain a platform of truth, not lies and bigotry. Freedom of speech also means freedom to tell the truth. In the old world, we tolerated "white lies," but our children should not be made to accept the premise that it's OK to lie. Our nation has found itself at a very dangerous crossroad, and if we continue on this path, soon, our young sons and daughters will accept the premise that lying is socially and morally acceptable. There is a moral imperative at stake, and the time has come when Congress and social media platforms should act. Otherwise, our country will display examples reminiscent of the days of the "Wild West."

The time has come for Congress to act on behalf of "We The People." Our leaders must implement standards and laws to ensure that our children and citizens will never be subjected to such a period of intellectual abuse. Democracy upholds truth and promotes facts, not alternative facts. Prestigious publications such as The *New York Times* or the *Washington Post* regularly publish apologies when they publish incorrect information. Therefore, cable TV and social media should be held to the same standards.

Chapter 12

The Ivy League Connection

Harvard and Yale Universities are prestigious institutions of learning. I was not fortunate, savvy enough, or wealthy enough to attend either institution. I was never a product of the meritocracy. Ted Cruz and Josh Hawley are products of Ivy League education and products of meritocracy. These so-called brilliant men were cheerleaders for the January 6 insurrection against America and Congress, a revered institution where both men serve. Ironically, Cruz led the insurrection immediately across from a building that he once served as a law clerk. Previously, he was even mentioned as a future Supreme Court justice. His chances of receiving future consideration for such a high office are now next to zero. A man who encourages others to break the law cannot be considered a candidate to uphold the law. The same holds for Hawley, whose predicted bright future in the Republican party is now tarnished.

Politicians should not mobilize an army of their citizens based on lies and misrepresentation of facts to damage our democracy. They should instead peacefully mobilize out of concern for the good of their citizens and not themselves. Following Cruz's dismal state of play in the insurrection, in the middle of a crippling emergency in his state, he and his family and friends left his desperate constituents for a vacation in Mexico. Cruz only returned from Mexico when he was photographed boarding a flight to Cancun, Mexico. As usual, Cruz lied about this encounter. During this emergency, people in Texas were burning furniture to generate heat to melt snow to flush toilets, and scrambling to secure drinking water, a phenomenon that was indeed happening in America. While the people of Texas suffered, their Senator escaped with his family to Mexico for sun and fun.

Cruz's actions have brought into focus the actual value of the much-hyped Ivy Leaguer status. Smart men and women would not continue to make dumb mistakes. In another instance, Cruz and his Republican friends tried to blame the recent power problems caused by a nor-easter on renewable energy. However, they knew that renewables constituted only 7 percent of Texas' power supply. One wonders whether Cruz graduated Summa Cum Laude in "Lying not under oath." Cruz and many of his colleagues seem to be at war with the truth and find it painful to tell the truth.

Even after the Congress was attacked, both men actively supported the insurrection, promoting lies and falsehood. Given their behavior, it appears that the education at both Harvard and Yale did not include "common sense." Both men likely skipped the lectures on ethics and social responsibility. Robert Green Ingersoll said, "It is a thousand times better to have common sense without education than to have education without common sense." I cannot conceive that these two great institutions' curriculum was devoid of ethics and social responsibility. Based on Cruz and Hawley's actions, I believe that both men collectively have done significant damage to the reputation and security of the U.S.

Ivy League technocrats and wealthy individuals dominate Congress. Their primary interest is self-preservation and power, and therefore have no interest in serving "We the People." The American public should seek candidates who have the people's interests at heart and not their selfish interests. However, we should elect candidates who are not controlled or manipulated by special interest groups. We need elected officials who are not dependent on large donations or desire to use representational politics as a stepping stone to higher offices. We need more Tip O'Neils and fewer of the Cruzs, Grahams, McConnells, and Hawleys.

Chapter 13

Violence in America

There is no mystery why teenagers and young adults turn to violence. More than 10 million children in the United States live in poverty and are deprived of the necessary resources and advancement opportunities. This is a discussion that our country needs to have. Because of their status, teenagers and young adults become easy prey for the master manipulators in our country. There is an idiom that states, "The devil finds work for idle hands." Children raised under deprived conditions are known to develop health problems, ultimately affecting their educational performance and causing them to complete fewer years in school. Fewer years in school usually results in securing lower-paying jobs. As a society, we must focus on getting relief for our teenagers and young adults from this terrible situation, helping them avoid the temptation to turn to violence as a last resort. Only then can we begin to see the light at the end of the tunnel.

Violence is a product of social inequalities. According to the U.S. Census Bureau, the official poverty rate in 2019 was 10.5 percent, representing more than 33 million from a population of 331 million. With the federal minimum wage at $7.25 per hour as of January 2021, U.S. citizens continue to have difficulty supporting their very existence. While not supporting any excuse for violence, these conditions can be described as putting live coal in an unextinguished fire pit. An undisturbed fire pit with no new energy sources will slowly die, and the remaining remnants of coal are unlikely to reignite. However, any attempt to add fuel to this fire pit while active will result in dire consequences, and that's what Trump, Cruz, and the company did.

A protest is a form of discourse. Protest is a process that allows us to communicate our agreement or disagreement regarding a specific or a series of mutually shared issues. However, the protest should only occur after we have collectively exhausted the channels of communication. Violence of any kind cannot be accepted or tolerated in our society. Peaceful protest cannot be associated with the burning of public or private property. When we destroy public or private property, it is the citizens who we claim to protect who are most affected. However, we cannot look the other way when law enforcement guns down scores of unarmed young Black men and women. Law enforcement is the same group that has sworn to protect our citizens. Therefore, we must work with government entities and the community to hold law enforcement accountable whenever they cross the line.

Countries such as France have suggested that violent outbreaks in that country are influenced by American culture and behavior. In many respects, this statement is true because we have watched lawlessness spin out of control over the years. Further, for better or for worse, many geographical regions of the world usually emulate the behaviors of the United States.

In an op-ed, Paul Krugman cited the Department of Homeland Security's April 2009 internal memo that warned that right-wing extremism was on the rise and had a growing potential for violence. Donald Trump became president and decided to hold on to power indefinitely by supporting and promoting right-wing extremism. His sentiments were fashioned by the man he most admires, Vladimir Putin. Trump deduced that through authoritarian means, he might control the U.S. Treasury and the Justice Department, including the F.B.I. These institutions would also be used to satisfy Trump's ego.

The U.S. Constitution, unlike Russia, does not allow the military to conduct active engagements in the 50 states; Trump then turned to right-wing activists to fill the void. To make this a reality, he used social media to wake up dormant societal evils and misgivings and unleash them on Americans. Trump did not create social unrest or violence; he simply used the tools available to achieve his objectives.

Trump advocated for the mistreatment of citizens by the police. He promoted racial division and homophobia, to name a few, and Americans left themselves vulnerable to a known bigot. Congress also bears responsibility for violence in America.

For years, the Republican members of Congress resisted sensible gun control legislation. Even after our kids and citizens were gunned down in cities and schools across the U.S., our politicians failed to address these problems. They were unable to justify why assault weapons, guns designed for war, were necessary to be carried on the streets of America. The Republican members of Congress succumbed to the National Rifle Association in exchange for a few dollars under the table. Congress and the local jurisdictions discounted the killings of black citizens, a phenomenon that created the Black Lives Matter (B.L.M.) movement, among others. B.L.M. might be the new kid on the block, but before starting B.L.M., activists like Martin Luther King Jr., John Lewis, Rev. Al Sharpton, Jessie Jackson, and other notables registered their opposition to how these matters were dealt with.

It is interesting to note that Americans can individually own up to 10 guns while men in combat are not so equipped. Truth About Guns estimates that Americans have more than 300 million guns and 12 trillion rounds of ammunition, enough to kill every man, woman, and child several times over. The central question is, which war are we getting ready to fight? In the last decade, we seem to use our array of firepower to intimidate each other instead of having civilized exchanges of ideas or hold discussions to settle our differences. We have suddenly forgotten that we can silence our critics with the power of conversation instead of resorting to the power of intimidation and violence.

Chapter 14

Signs of the Times-High Season

Most politicians behave like used car salesmen. The average citizen can deduce that election time is near because all politicians escape from their cocoons, attend various church services in their community, visit community centers, kiss babies, and greet the elderly. Of note, in what I call "High Season," some politicians attend church services every two or four years and, in most instances, are never regular visitors or members. For the next 12 to 48 months, the electorates are left to fend for themselves until the next election cycle.

Once the "High Season" is over, members of Congress and local counterparts return to serve lobbyists and special interest groups. Once elections are held and the winners decided, fundraising activities begin almost immediately. Politicians spend more time raising funds for the next election and in discussions with lobbyists and therefore have little time to service constituency needs. Moreover, the Senate is the premier club of wealthy individuals. As of December 2020, over one-half of the members of Congress were millionaires.

In response to the January 6, 2021 insurrection and the associated impeachment of Donald J. Trump, his second impeachment in less than three months, U.S. Senate leaders could not find the courage to serve justice. Regardless of the evidence that was presented, they were afraid to act. Their actions have left an indelible stain on America that will change how the world perceives a once-great nation. A nation is not considered great because of its wealth but because of its humanity and trustworthiness. The Gingrich Republican party started the work of destroying the fabric of our country. Trump inherited the blueprint and the tools of destruction. With the help of McConnell, Cruz, and others, he advanced an agenda of self-aggrandizement. The long-term results of his behavior will reverberate in the hall of this nation for years to come.

Chapter 15

The Role of the Church in Politics

Churches, synagogues, temples, and other houses of worship have increasingly engaged in American politics, much to their peril and despite the constitutional requirement for the separation of church and state. Over the last century, the church has lost its way by abandoning its core competencies and has lost its respect and independence. Churches have become more focused on a predetermined political agenda rather than focusing on helping the poor and needy as Christ advocated. Today's church either employs lobbyists or assists lobbyists and politicians in driving specific agendas. Many of these agendas are not sanctioned by the church's membership but instead driven by the church's hierarchy and influential contributors. The church is not just a meeting place; it's a place where one seeks the truth and spiritual guidance. It is supposed to be a place of healing and reconciliation and not a place that encourages division.

In many instances, politicians invite themselves to church services and are openly welcomed by priests, rabbis, and pastors. Leaders of the bodies and establishments make this accommodation a means of staying connected, with the intention of "calling in the chips" sometime in the future. This quid-pro-quo arrangement, among other things, has consistently weakened the church's standing with congregants and contributes to a loss of interest in the church. The result is a dwindling membership and closed or bankrupt churches.

The church has always been a place where people go for solace.

Still, church leaders recognizing their congregants' vulnerability use every occasion to manipulate and inculcate individuals seeking relief. Church leaders spend an excessive amount of time curry-favoring politicians instead of attending to their congregants' spiritual needs. Some pastors encourage the neediest individuals to give their last dollar while they maintain lofty lifestyles. These are all behaviors that contribute to social and economic discontent.

Some churches use the Sunday morning service to advance political agendas and to overlay their political views on the congregation. In the northeast, there are several instances where prominent politicians are pastors. In some cases, pastors who have served and maintain ties with Congress have been awarded lucrative positions in academia and organizations run by state and local governments. Business dealings of this caliber should not be allowed, given the potential conflict of interests. A grave disservice is done to our system of government and our religious organizations by having these associations and securing these appointments.

It is a known fact that white Protestant Christians have long been affiliated with white supremacists. Pre Trump, these fractions had been operating incognito, much to the detriment of our civil society. The church has expanded its reach in cooperating with groups like QAnon and formed a religious right movement supporting their selfish ideology. Since the January 6 insurrection, the religious right has been silent. Not a word has been spoken condemning the actions of those who were involved in this destructive act. Most mega-churches that were quite vocal during the political theatre hosted by Trump have not used their bully pulpit to encourage members to get vaccinated against the COVID-19 disease. COVID-19 has significantly affected the operation of the local church. While some churches were active in promoting vaccinations, others remain silent and indifferent to the situation. One would deduce that it would be in the church's best interest to encourage and promote the vaccination of the people in the community.

Chapter 16

Ethics and Politics

There is a lack of convergence between ethics and politics in the modern Congress. There is virtually no transparency in the political process. Ordinary people are denied the right to walk the halls of Congress, while lobbyists roam the corridors with unlimited access. Politicians have written laws to allow insider trading for members of Congress. At the same time, ordinary Americans are sent to prison for doing the same. History has taught us that Congress will never learn from the mistakes of past members.

Over the years, Americans have seen several of their elected officials sent to prison because of various financial and trading schemes. Members of Congress should be subjected to the same rules that many of us who work in the financial service industry must follow. In the past, a governor from a Midwestern state was given a lengthy prison term in his attempt to seek monetary compensation for selling the Illinois Senate seat that the then-Senator Obama vacated. In other instances, politicians have hired prominent lawyers who have succeeded in getting acquittals on their behalf.

The U.S. Office of Congressional Ethics is charged with reviewing allegations of misconduct. The Senate Select Committee on Ethics deals with ethics matters within the Senate. But the rules that set the boundaries on congressional behavior need to be re-examined. The guidelines regarding the ethical conduct of the elected members of Congress are governed by either the House Ethics Manual or the

Senate Ethics Manual. The manual is created and revised by the House and Senate committees on ethics.

But these two committees are not necessarily independent of the body. They must operate within the confines of the committees' arcane rules. Americans should therefore demand a constitutional amendment to force the creation of an independent national commission on ethics, with each commission member serving a five - eight-year term. Members of this commission should be appointed by the president of the United States and approved by a majority vote of the Senate. Under this proposal, the Senate should not be allowed to filibuster such nominations and require a simple majority. The House committee should adopt a similar process. A majority vote of this committee should also establish the rules. Such a committee would bring much-needed credibility to congressional ethics.

Chapter 17

The Role of Government

Government has many roles in the U.S. economy. The main reason for having a government is to centrally provide low-cost services to its people. Good government assesses the long and short-term risks of their economy and, therefore, proceeds to build and maintain the necessary infrastructure to respond to local and national issues, especially in a crisis.

Some individuals believe that government should not be involved in providing services that can be provided more efficiently by the private sector and at a lower cost. In most countries, public service is subsidized by revenue from taxation. In the United States, some states not only support other states but subsidize the federal government. As a result, this causes regional imbalances and can create what is known as high-tax jurisdictions. These imbalances will be challenging to address since representatives from the low-tax jurisdictions will never agree to an increase in their contribution to the U.S. Treasury. Similarly, the states are in the same dilemma, as some cities receive more aid than they contribute to the state treasury.

A broad spectrum of people worldwide is becoming impatient with government institutions, as the government fails to deliver services to address the needs of the people they represent. As a result, people become affiliated with ethnic, cultural, religious, political, and even hate groups. With governments under pressure to deliver more

64

services without commensurate revenue increases, people tend to resort to the kinds of behaviors that have created underlining chaos that we have witnessed recently. The recent series of events has contributed to the erosion of law and order and our democracy.

Like a major corporation, the government spends and earns income from various sources. Government consumes goods and services and employs a significant portion of our citizens. Federal, state, and local governments raise funds through taxes, fees, and borrowing from the public domain. The government often borrows money from the public by selling securities, such as bonds. Governments also spend money via contracts with private businesses, procure goods and services, or funding social programs that benefit the public.

Governments are responsible for providing services such as law enforcement, military defense, fire and roads, education, social services, water, and environmental protection. In providing certain services, governments collect taxes and fees and charge for many services they provide to the public. Like many members of the public, government entities sometimes tend to spend more than they make, and this can lead to higher taxes or a reduction in critical services. Unless there is full accountability, government can cease to be an asset and may become a burdensome liability on its citizens.

Chapter 18

Big Government

How big should the government be? I believe that government should be as big as necessary because no one-size-fits-all government will work effectively. The government's size and scope should adjust like a rubber band, expand when warranted, and contract when the demand for services decreases. The size and complexity of the government of the 1930s could not function in 2021, notwithstanding a population of more than 300 million people and an explosion in technological advancement. Politicians blame the problems of our country on government and promote a negative narrative. There is nothing wrong with government. Everything is wrong with the people who control the purse strings that keep the government operational.

There are many issues in the 20th and 21st centuries, the most pronounced being the current pandemic. You may recall that the government was slow in addressing this critical issue because of infighting, coupled with the government's inability to accept responsibility and a lack of political will. It takes a big government to run a big and powerful country such as the U.S. Similarly, Exxon and B.P. are as big as they needed to support their business activities and complexity.

Comparably, Amazon is a supersize company that continues to grow to meet its customers' ever-expanding demand worldwide. Amazon, U.P.S., and FedEx cannot rely on the horses and buggies of the 1930s and abacuses to expand commerce, and the U.S. government is in the same position. Those who complain excessively about the government's size should consider the appropriateness of Walmart running the military or having the states respond to national emergencies. We have seen attempts by the federal government to delegate COVID-19 responsibilities to the states. This experiment was a dismal failure.

It is not a big government that has failed. Failure results from incompetent and untrustworthy state legislators, members of Congress, and the executive branch. They have been unable to address the issues that matter most. The technocrats that keep the government operational are working above and beyond the call of duty. They are operating with 18th-century processes and technology. In some instances, the government tries to merge out-of-date procedures with modern systems, much to their dismay. We cannot and should not place people in government if they don't believe in government. Consequently, the people of this country should seize the moment and send the non-performers and those who loathe the government home.

The federal workforce under Trump became smaller and unhappier. As a result, vital services were affected. Tax collection fell because of the lack of enforcement, even as the Trump Administration cut taxes for the rich, a movie that we have seen before under Ronald Regan. This move may provide short-term benefits for a few. But in the long run, it will be a prescription for disaster. We should not borrow money to fund a tax cut.

The Trump Administration launched a program to reduce the federal workforce through firings and other actions to force workers to leave the government. As a result, critical agencies like the State Department, Homeland Security, Education, and Labor are at risk of not performing as mandated, especially during a crisis. Many workers were fired because they were unfairly viewed as part of the "Deep State." We must squash idle talk about the wrongs of the governmental apparatus and move to allocate funding to improve operational effectiveness. If we want our government to work efficiently, the executive branch and Congress must provide the necessary financing to procure modern processes and systems. Similarly, we must also provide adequate training for those who provide services to the nation. Only then will we be able to certify that there is an efficient process in place.

Chapter 19

Club Capitol Hill

Club Capitol Hill is a majestic place, a place where personal and political dreams are realized. We Americans are proud of the edifice that our founding fathers left us. Still, we grieve at what this remarkable structure has become. It has become a place where members settle political scores while pretending to be representing the people of this country. Once a new member arrives at this majestic palace, built for 550 kings and queens, decked with crystal chandeliers and numerous arcane rules and processes, ensure that a dysfunctional system remains in place. Members usually serve well beyond retirement age, some displaying physical distress as they commute through the labyrinth of tunnels on their way to the floors of Senate and House and House of Representatives.

Over the years, members of Congress have built an expansive city partially to prevent easy access and to cement their exclusivity. They created an elaborate subway system that provides transportation to various office buildings, aka - mini-palaces. Yet, New York City, with more than 9 million people, still does not have a direct ride to J.F.K. Airport, one of the world's busiest airports. Once an individual gets a membership to this exclusive club, they become de-facto members for life. Suppose a member chooses to leave or is removed by their constituents. In that case, they are awarded extraordinary benefits at the expense of uninsured Americans. Ironically, some of the same members voted against healthcare reform "Obamacare" and later pledged to repeal the Affordable Care Act.

Generally, members are required to wait two years before they can officially lobby Congress. In many instances, as members leave Congress, they maintain unfettered access to their former colleagues and often use this influence to dictate public policy, as if they never left the government. This access level makes it quite profitable for the former members of Congress. They collect lucrative fees billed to corporate clients and high net-worth individuals. These lucrative under-the-table gentleman's arrangements are among the significant reasons why much-needed political and other reforms have never seen the light of day. But "We the People" have immense power. We have authority that was given to us by our Constitution. We must use this power to force change by changing the way Congress does its business. Change is also necessary to ensure that Congress passes strong ethical laws to protect our democracy.

Corporate giants and mid-size companies pay lobbyists approximately $3 billion each year to influence congressional decisions. A single company with the necessary resources can dictate how and if a single bill becomes law. These companies influence political outcomes regarding national issues, not just with lobbying efforts but also with significant cash contributions to individual politicians and political parties, directly or indirectly through Political Action Committees (P.A.C.). Recent attempts by the late Senator John McCain to introduce legislation to bring some credibility to Congress were significantly defeated, primarily by members of his own party.

Americans can make a difference if they organize, target, and change the congressional status quo. The voters in this country did not intend to elect a Congress that provides the breeding ground for power brokers. They elected men and women who are supposed to represent their interests in Congress.

Current congressional leaders behave in a manner akin to being a member of the executive branch. Sometimes, the conflicts force them to self-destruct, like the tapes used to introduce the "Mission Impossible" series or the James Bond 007 movies. It might be appropriate to assume that the modern-day Congress is squarely in the entertainment business while treating law-making as a part-time activity. As a result, Congress conducts extensive political maneuvering while passing fewer laws in shorter sessions and providing an inadequate appropriation for the suitable projects.

Members of Congress have become so angry at the very system they have created, and they blame others for the hazards and accept no blame for their actions. Each day, they conduct political theatre. I am not aware that we have corporate headquarters where employees can break during working hours and relax in the company's swimming pool. The result is that the people of this country are left disappointed with congressional performance. Similarly, they experience reduced services, higher costs, low wages, and broken and expensive educational, healthcare, and housing systems. The need is great, and temperatures are rising. Congress must have a dialogue with the people of this country and entertain the proper political discourse to calm the oceans of overcharged emotions.

Chapter 20

Congressional Discipline

The Federal government in 2019 will collect $3.5 trillion in taxes, 16 percent of G.D.P., and spend $4.4 trillion, 21 percent of G.D.P. after a six-decade low in tax revenue. Over the same period, there has been a high in spending. The world's largest economy cannot continue to be run on borrowed money, policies that both political parties share the responsibility for creating. These policies have now brought our country close to the economic and financial precipice. Being the largest user of our tax dollars, many Americans feel that the military should be subjected to strict budgetary rules and strict fiscal discipline. Taxation ought to be a part of the solution because there is no free lunch.

The country needs to collect more revenue from those capable of paying more while bringing some relief to the middle class. Failure to address America's economic disparity will provide the fuel for civil disobedience, much to our country's detriment. Some leaders in the private sector are leading the way in addressing social and economic inequalities. In contrast, others who earn millions of dollars still refuse to pay their fair share of taxes. In a recent interview with CNN, Bill Gates shared that he paid $10 billion in taxes in 2019 and is willing to pay $20 billion if he has to. This is quite noble, considering that thousands of wealthy Americans pay little or no taxes. The ex-president paid no taxes for several years.

This brings me to the point where I will suggest that there is "enough manna" (using a biblical term) to go around. There is no need for us to position ourselves to collect the crumbs from the table. Under our current system, the first one to the table eats, and the last one to the table gets eaten for dinner. I assume that Gates knows this to be accurate, and perhaps that's why he has dedicated his life and wealth to solving some of the world's most challenging problems.

The conundrum remains that Republicans are bitterly opposed to supporting new taxes, and Democrats have failed to fund social programs' rationalization and reform. As a result, as a nation, we will not achieve our ultimate potential. While the political heavy-weights continue their slugfest, the country is experiencing a recession, hunger, high unemployment levels, and homeowners wrestling with underwater mortgages. The public needs our politicians to make progress, lift our people's economic spirits, and move expeditiously to prevent continued social and economic unrest. Politicians should view the "Occupy Wall Street" protests held all over the country and the world as a sign that Americans will not sit back and watch our government preside over their demise.

Chapter 21

The U.S. Supreme Court

The U.S. Supreme Court is the most potent arm of the judiciary. The Supreme Court's checks and balances can be implemented only by constitutional amendment, which is extremely difficult, if not impossible, to achieve in this politically charged and divided environment. For many years, the Supreme Court has become uniquely ideological. In the last four years, the Senate's majority leader publicly engineered a plan to install only conservative justices on the court. As of this writing, he has successfully installed three conservative justices. These justices view cases presented to them through the eyes of their preferred ideological lenses, instead of reflecting the direction offered by the Constitution and in association with the majority of citizens that they represent. They often argue that they follow the Constitution but instead interpret the Constitution through their preferred ideological and political lenses.

The U.S. Supreme Court, by its action, is somewhat responsible for the current political crisis in America. The court has allowed unregulated money to be introduced in political campaigns, giving the wealthy and well-connected carte blanche to influence election results. They affect the government's operations, much to the dismay of the majority of our citizens. They have not reigned in the abuse of our electoral process where some states have gone to the extreme of limiting our citizens' rights to vote. They have made statements that suggested that they would consider terminating the laws that guarantee a woman's right to choose a position that is not in line with most Americans. These inequities, among others, have provided fodder to those who need the perfect excuse to participate in illegal activities and vitriolic speech. Justices of the court must start "listening" to the Constitution and the people's voice and not their voices and prejudices.

The size of the court is set by law, not by the Constitution. In response to Republican power grab in 2016 and 2020 that led to establishing a clear majority of conservative judges on the Supreme Court, President Biden has appointed a 36-person commission to make recommendations on the restructuring of the Supreme Court. Within the commission structure are various working groups. The president has mandated that one of the working groups focus on the Supreme Court's role in the constitutional system. A vital element of the focus will be on the court's role in being the final arbiter of significant issues.

One of the proposals is for Congress to strip the court of jurisdiction over specific topics and create a process for lawmakers to override court decisions. Other committee members would address the length of service, including a recommendation for mandatory retirement age on older justices. Similarly, House members have introduced a bill to expand the size of the Supreme Court to 13 members instead of the current nine members. Although probably necessary in responding to Republican actions, these moves will further inflame the current political landscape.

Chapter 22

Conclusion

I hope you would take a moment to reflect on the discussions and observations that I advanced through this media. Most importantly, I hope that you have benefitted from them. I recognized that it's quite easy to read through these pages, understand the concepts and arguments and finally decide to do nothing to advance fairness and respect for other points of view. Ignoring societal issues hoping it would disappear like the flue is never a responsible position to take. We will always be rewarded (good or bad) for the choices that we make in life. We can choose to take the necessary steps to bring back a sense of normalcy and civility to our country or sit back and let it burn to the ground.

The element of fairness and trust are essential ingredients for a democracy to function and succeed. Everyone in the democracy must believe that there is a system in place that will ensure equity across gender, ethnicity, and religion. It is equally important that every voice be heard and not ignored. Those in government must cease representing themselves and return to representing the electors. We should make every attempt to restart peaceful conversations, disagree if we must, and agree on the issues that will advance our citizens and our country.

Conflicts occur when the wants of the people go contrary to the desires of our leaders. Unless the people and political leaders learn to compromise for the good of the people and the country, we will not experience long-term success. Different points of view cannot be independently satisfied without some level of compromise. Compromise entails coordination and collaboration, especially when both parties cannot independently achieve a specific goal or outcome.

With collective action and compromise, we can, as a nation, solve the political nightmare that has plagued our country for too long. First, we must commit ourselves to be factual, honest, decent, empathetic, and understanding others' needs. We must be trustworthy, recognizing that we are all equal under God and our Constitution. We must never let our citizens feel that they have been ignored because all of us are God's creation. Our education, status, or wealth do not render any of us as being better than others. America can again become a beacon of light to the world. These qualities will promote practical political discourse, defuse conflicts, and promote a just society that can never again be seen as a Nation Under Siege.

ACKNOWLEDGMENTS

This publication has been in the works for over two years. However, as I got closer to the ending of 2019, it became clear that it was time to document my thoughts and concepts in the public forum. A brief discussion with my immediate and extended family prompted me to proceed with this project, despite my busy schedule and corporate demands.

I want to extend my appreciation to Dr. Dennis V. Burke for his advice and editorial comments and suggestions during this process. Dr. Burke is a scholar-practitioner who studies emotional intelligence and the influence of principle-based decision-making on leadership and managerial success. Dr. Burke is a leadership coach and university lecturer in South Carolina. Dr. Burke is the author of several publications.

My sincere thanks to Cindy Beatty of Positive Proof for providing valuable suggestions in finalizing the manuscript to meet my self-imposed deadlines.

ABOUT THE AUTHOR

Adrian L. Lawrence is an accomplished Finance and Regulatory Executive with many years of experience in the Financial Services industry. Mr. Lawrence holds a BBA in Finance, an MBA in Technology Management. Mr. Lawrence is a Commissioned Bank Examiner, Certified Information Systems Auditor (CISA), Certification in Risk Management Assurance (CRMA), and is Certified in Risk and Information Systems Control (CRISC). Mr. Lawrence has previously served as Board Member in several Non-Profit organizations.

www.ingramcontent.com/pod-product-compliance
Lightning Source LLC
Chambersburg PA
CBHW050600280326
41933CB00011B/1928